Natural Disasters

SHERRI RINKEL-MacKAY •
PAT CLIFFORD • JUDY MARTIN

Editorial Board
David Booth • Joan Green • Jack Booth

Steck Vaughn™
A Harcourt Achieve Imprint

10801 N. Mopac Expressway
Building # 3
Austin, TX 78759
1.800.531.5015

Steck-Vaughn is a trademark of Harcourt Achieve Inc. registered in the United States of America and/or other jurisdictions. All inquiries should be mailed to Harcourt Achieve Inc., P.O. Box 27010, Austin, TX 78755.

Rubicon © 2006 Rubicon Publishing Inc.
www.rubiconpublishing.com

All rights reserved. No part of this publication may be reproduced or transmitted in any form or by any means, electronic or mechanical, including photocopying, recording, taping, or any information storage and retrieval system, without permission in writing from the copyright owner. BOLDPRINT is a trademark of BOLDPRINT BOOKS.

Project Editors: Miriam Bardswich, Kim Koh
Editorial Assistant: Lori McNeelands
Art/Creative Director: Jennifer Drew-Tremblay
Assistant Art Director: Jen Harvey
Designer: Jeanette Debusschere

Natural Disasters
13: ISBN 978-1-41902-402-3
10: ISBN 1-419024-02-7

CONTENTS

4 **Introduction**

6 **Quake Shakes 'Frisco**
Check out this report on an Earth-shattering quake.

9 **Measuring Shakes**
An informational piece on ways to detect earthquakes.

10 **Quake Facts**
Unbelievable earthquake statistics.

12 **Pelee Awakes**
A true story about a volcano that wiped out an entire town.

15 **The Hurricane**
See how a poet can paint a picture with words.

16 **Hurricane Hoopla**
Read this report to get the lowdown on hurricanes.

20 **Cyclone!**
Dorothy's not in Kansas any more. Enjoy this excerpt from the novel, *The Wizard of Oz*.

22 **Disaster at Pine Lake**
This graphic story will have you thinking twice about your next trip to the cottage.

26 **Fighting Forest Fires**
Check out this interview in which firefighters describe how they tame raging forest fires.

32 **Flood of '94**
A touching poem about one woman's flood experience.

34 **Flood Facts**
Read this article to find out about floodwaters.

35 **River of Sorrow**
Read this report to learn all about China's Yellow River, which has killed millions over the years.

38 **Millions of Lives at Risk**
Life during a drought can be devastating. This report explains why.

41 **Avalanche!**
Read this report to find out why an avalanche is such a deadly force of nature.

44 **Wave of Terror**
Imagine waves traveling as fast as 450 mph. Read this description of a tsunami.

46 **Thai Survivors Face the Future**
For these children, getting in the water is a nightmare. Find out why in this article.

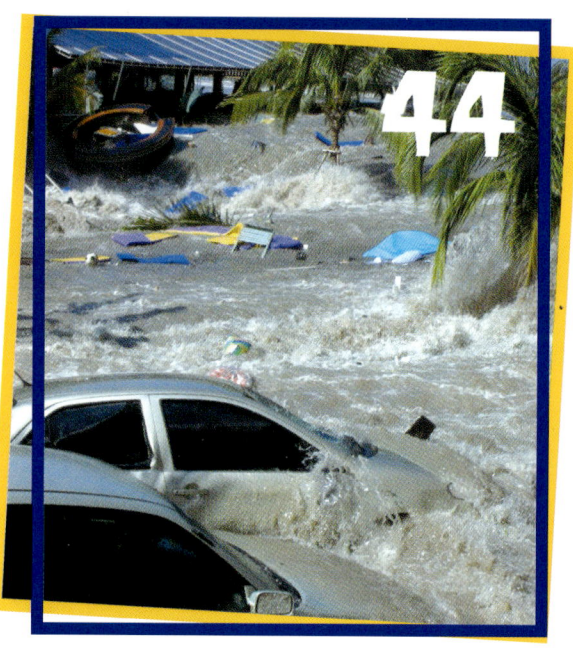

PLUS SAFETY & SURVIVAL TIPS

Human beings can change and control many things, but never the awesome powers of Mother Nature.

Taiwanese Army rescue workers hurry to find survivors of an earthquake that killed more than 2,000 people in September 1999.

QUAKE SHAKES 'FRISCO

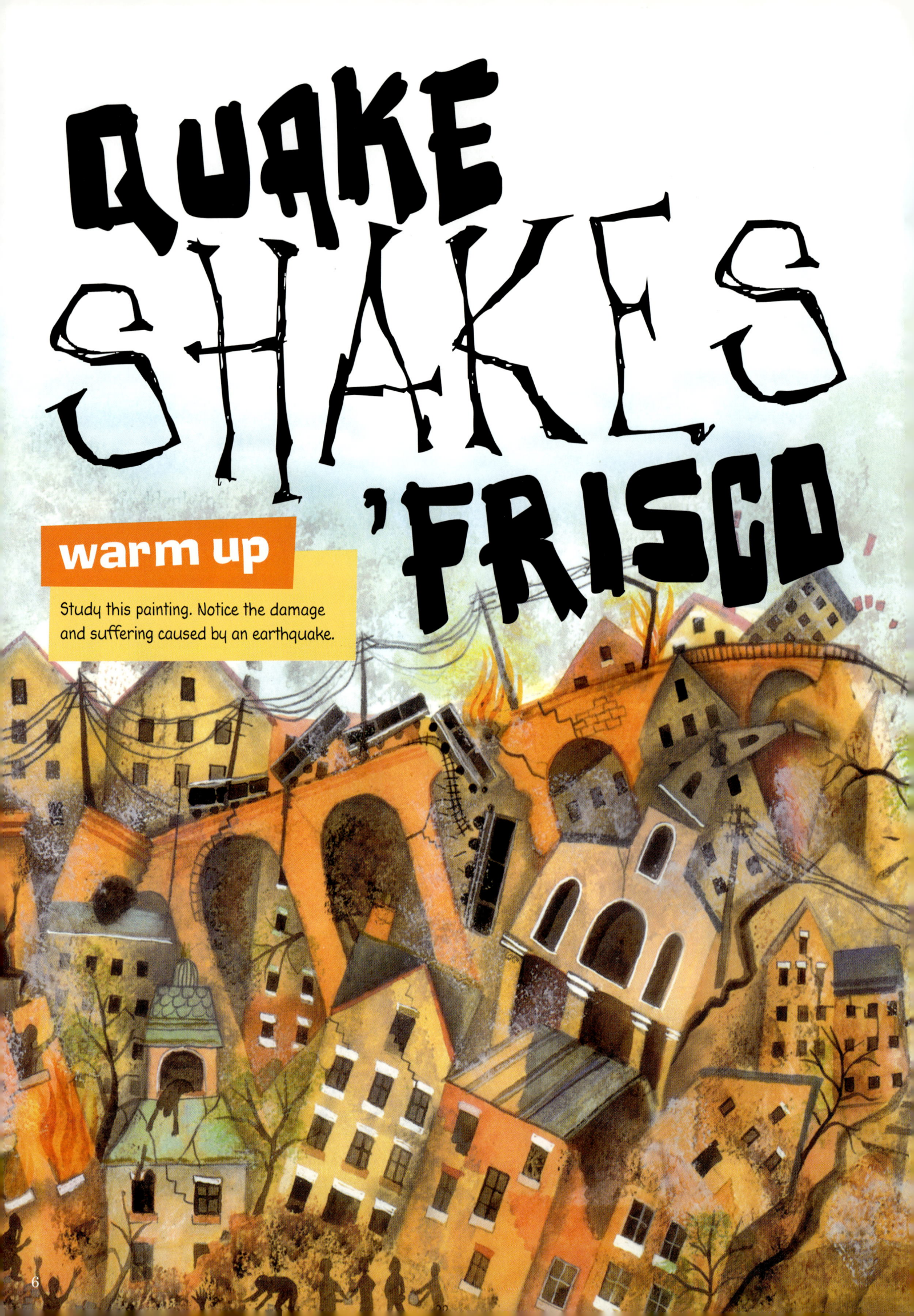

warm up

Study this painting. Notice the damage and suffering caused by an earthquake.

San Francisco's baseball fans were thrilled. On October 17, 1989, their home team was ready to play the third game of the World Series. About 62,000 people were packed inside Candlestick Park (a stadium). The game was about to begin when suddenly everything began to rock.

"Oh my God, we're having an earthquake!" gasped the announcer. When the shaking stopped 15 seconds later, everyone in the stadium was fine. They cheered wildly. They didn't realize that other parts of the city had not fared so well.

Several older homes in the Marina District toppled. Some caught fire. Most residents managed to escape, but a few were trapped in the wreckage. Fire crews quickly took command of the situation. In three hours, the fires were out. Experts explained that the Marina District suffered more damage than other areas because its soft soil had turned soupy during the shaking.

Even worse, the multi-level Cypress Freeway collapsed. The upper deck crashed into the lower deck. Emergency crews struggled to reach survivors, all the time aware that earthquake aftershocks (small earthquakes) could knock down the damaged structure. While they managed to pull some people from their crushed cars, dozens of others died.

wreckage: *damaged buildings*

CHECKPOINT
What would you do if you heard this announcement? Have you ever been in a situation where there was a similar warning?

CHECKPOINT
What do you think builders think about when they are planning and building offices, homes, and roadways in areas where earthquakes might occur?

Workers check the damage to the Cypress Freeway on October 19, 1989, two days after it collapsed as a result of the earthquake.

Rescue dogs search for survivors in the Marina District of San Francisco.

wrap up

Using the information and the photographs in this article, write a newspaper report on the San Francisco earthquake. Include a headline.

MEASURING SHAKES

A seismograph measures and records the waves or vibrations from earthquakes that travel through the Earth. The time, locations, and strength of an earthquake can be determined by the data recorded by a seismograph.

In the year 132 A.D., a Chinese scientist called Zhang Heng made the first tool for detecting earthquakes. The instrument could detect even the slightest earthquakes. It could also identify the direction the earthquake had come from based on which toad's mouth a ball dropped into.

Today, scientists use complex, high-tech instruments to measure the Earth's vibration patterns. Modern seismographs can measure the Earth's waves with much more precision. They also monitor much larger areas of land.

This is Zhang Heng's invention. When an earthquake began, the balls in the dragons' mouths would shake. As the quake became stronger, the balls would drop from the dragons' mouths into the toads' mouths.

FYI

The Richter scale, introduced by Charles Richter in 1935, measures the force of earthquakes on a scale of one to nine. An earthquake measuring over seven on the Richter scale can cause serious damage.

This is a modern-day seismograph.

wrap up

Use the Internet to find out how many earthquakes over seven on the Richter scale happened in the past year. Show each location and the size of the quake on a chart.

QUAKE FACTS

The San Andreas Fault runs through California. It's almost 700 miles long. Not all earthquakes are dangerous — many small earthquakes occur along the fault several times a month. These earthquakes don't usually hurt anyone or destroy property.

The strongest earthquake recorded in the United States happened in Alaska on March 27, 1964. The quake measured 9.2 on the Richter scale and 125 people died. In some places the ground surface was raised or lowered more than 28 feet!

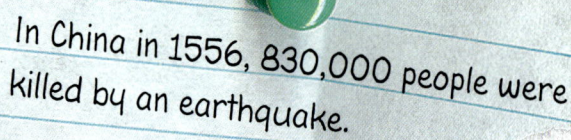

Over one million earthquakes occur around the world every year.

In China in 1556, 830,000 people were killed by an earthquake.

In 1960, the largest earthquake ever recorded happened in Chile. The quake killed over 6,000 people, and caused a tsunami that actually killed people in Hawaii and Japan. The earthquake measured 9.5 on the Richter scale.

tsunami: *giant wave caused by an underwater earthquake*

TSUNAMI HAZARD ZONE

IN CASE OF EARTHQUAKE, GO TO HIGH GROUND OR INLAND

➡️ If you are outdoors, move away from buildings, street lights, and utility wires.

➡️ If you're indoors during an earthquake, keep calm and take cover under a heavy table or desk. Be sure to stay away from glass (like windows or mirrors) or anything that could fall, like a bookcase.

➡️ If you are in a crowded public place, do not run for the doors or get into an elevator. Instead, take cover under something heavy.

➡️ Aftershocks will occur after an earthquake. If a building has been damaged during an earthquake, an aftershock may cause it to collapse.

collapse: fall down

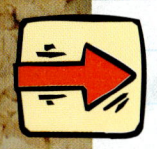

➡️ If you are inside and you smell gas or hear a loud hissing sound, open a window and get out of the building at once. Tell an adult right away. A gas line in your house may have been broken.

➡️ Always wear shoes after an earthquake. There could be broken glass on the ground.

STAYING SAFE IN A SHAKE

WEB CONNECTIONS

Check out the website **http://earthquake.usgs.gov/4kids**. Play one of the online games with a friend.

11

PELEE AWAKES

Martinique, Caribbean, 1902

It was nearly 8:00 AM, and the port of St. Pierre on the Caribbean island of Martinique was bustling. Sugar, rum, and bananas were being loaded onto ships, while rich French tourists strolled along the elegant streets. Local people worked in the heat of the orchards and plantations.

Yet people were leaving town. Some were waiting for boats to take them off the island. Others were leaving by road. They were nervous because the usually quiet Pelee was belching smoke and ashes.

An official report had said there was no danger. But this did not stop the fear that gripped the town, and Governor Mouttet sent guards to keep more people from leaving.

Leon, the local shoemaker, watched the people leaving. He had lived here all his life and knew there was no cause for alarm.

warm up

What do you know about volcanoes? Why do people live near active volcanoes?

CHECKPOINT

Can you believe every news report you hear? Do people make mistakes in reporting?

FYI

- Not everything about volcanoes is bad. The minerals from the ash and lava help plants grow.

- Geothermal power is heat that comes from inside the Earth and is carried to the surface by a volcano. This heat can be used to make electricity.

- Some metals and precious stones are made when minerals from a volcano melt and mix together.

- Volcanic mud is thought to have special healing powers.

In his jail cell, Auguste Ciparis wasn't concerned either. Locked away, without even a window, he knew nothing of events in the town.

Suddenly Mount Pelee exploded with a sound like a thousand cannons firing. A glowing cloud of hot steam, dust, and gas rolled down the mountain — heading straight for St. Pierre!

The suffocating air killed most people instantly. Some tried to escape, but they were overtaken by the rapidly moving cloud. It was so hot that it burst open the skulls and stomachs of people as they fled.

Leon staggered into his house, clutching his chest. His lungs were gripped with pain, and his skin was burning. He threw himself onto his bed, expecting to die. All around him things began to melt in the heat.

The streets ran with burning rum from flattened warehouses. Ships in the harbor capsized and sank as the fiery blast swept over them. In a matter of seconds, St. Pierre was reduced to a flaming ruin!

FYI

Prisoner Ciparis had been found guilty of murder and sentenced to death. He was one of two people who survived the volcano. Later he toured the world with the Barnum and Bailey Circus in a model of his prison cell.

wrap up

With a partner, write the script for a TV news report about this disaster. What are some of the ways you would describe the event?

WEB CONNECTIONS

Using the Internet, find out the warning signs that tell a volcano is about to erupt. Use the information in a poster titled: "Warning! Eruption Coming!"

SAFETY TIPS

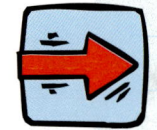

➡️ If you live in an area near a volcano, sit down with your family to create a disaster plan.

➡️ Stay inside to protect yourself from volcanic ash. Be sure to close all doors and windows. If lava flows begin, you will have to leave the building.

➡️ Cover your nose and mouth so that you don't breathe in ash.

➡️ Never go to watch an active volcano explode. The volcano is unpredictable. If there is ash in the air, avoid being *downwind* from the volcano.

downwind: in the path of oncoming wind

➡️ Watch for flying rocks and mudflows. Mudflows can move very fast. You will not be able to outrun a mudflow.

➡️ After an eruption, an adult should clear away any ash that may be on the roof. The ash is heavy and could cause the roof to collapse.

DANGER VOLCANO ERUPTING

WEB CONNECTIONS

Using the Internet, find out about the **"Ring of Fire"** around the Pacific Ocean. Share your information in a report to the class.

THE HURRICANE

By Luis Pales Matos
A Poem from Puerto Rico — translated by Alida Malkus

When the hurricane unfolds
Its fierce accordion of winds,
On the tip of its toes,
Agile dancer, it sweeps whirling
Over the carpeted surface of the sea
With the scattered branches of the palm.

wrap up

A metaphor is an imaginative way to compare two different things. How many metaphors can you find in this poem? Draw a picture of a hurricane based on the images created by the poet.

Agile: *flexible*

Hurricane Hoopla

warm up

What do you think a hurricane is? Have you ever been at a place where they have had a hurricane?

Hurricanes are powerful, dangerous storms that start over oceans. The strong winds cause damage to human life and property both on shore and at sea. If you live near the coast, you may have seen the damage first-hand. If you don't live near the coast, you probably have heard about it on television. But have you heard about the snake problem? Or the flying turtles? Hurricanes can cause some pretty strange stuff to happen.

In 1961, Hurricane Carla **ravaged** Texas City, with winds up to 145 miles per hour. It rained so hard that the town flooded. Some people were able to get away before the hurricane hit. Others weren't as lucky. After the hurricane, the people who remained ran into another problem. Snakes! Snakes were everywhere. Thousands of rattlesnakes slithered through the town. Because the town was so flooded, the snakes went to the only high land. Guess who else was there? The hurricane survivors! The snake problem is fairly common in hurricane-prone areas. People have to be very careful in areas like Texas City, where some snakes are poisonous.

ravaged: *devastated*

CHECKPOINT
What happened when this hurricane hit Texas?

CHECKPOINT
Notice that not only people head to high ground for safety.

Wind gusts during a hurricane are very dangerous. You often hear about heavy objects whirling through the air, or about buildings blowing over. Sometimes hurricane winds blow over entire towns. In 1935, two land turtles were caught in a hurricane. The turtles blew through the air for 20 miles. One turtle weighed 165 lb.! They blew across the top of the Gulf of Florida. As they skipped across the water, they pulled in their heads and legs. Their hard shells protected them. Scientists were amazed the turtles lived.

Other hurricane survivors have seen some pretty strange stuff. Some hurricanes have ripped up graveyards. People watched in horror as caskets floated down flooded roads!

Four major hurricanes slammed across the Atlantic coast during the 2004 hurricane season. The last time this happened was in 1886, when four hurricanes pounded the state of Texas.

ORDER	HURRICANE	WIND SPEEDS	CATEGORY
1.	Charley	145 mph	4
2.	Frances	100 mph	2
3.	Ivan	165 mph	5
4.	Jeanne	115 mph	3

*The Saffir-Simpson scale ranks hurricanes from one to five, according to their wind speeds and how much damage they could cause. One is the least amount of damage, and five is the highest.

According to meteorologist Stu Ostro of the Weather Channel, "Overall, this [2004 hurricane season] has been a very destructive and costly hurricane season. The official totals are not in yet, but this will likely go down as the costliest hurricane season on record in the U.S."

wrap up

1. Choose one hurricane from the table and research the damage it caused.
2. Why do you think hurricanes are given names? How could you find out?

FYI

1,600 people were killed in Haiti by Hurricane Ivan in 2004.

➡️ Listen to a radio or television for weather updates. Stay in touch with your neighbors about evacuation orders.

evacuation: leaving a place

➡️ Plan a place to meet your family in case you are separated during a disaster. Get your disaster supply kit and extra water now! Remind your parents to make sure there is enough gas in the car in case you have to leave.

➡️ If the wind stops, do not leave your safe place. A pause in the wind could be the eye of the storm, which means the wind will come again.

➡️ Remember to always STAY INDOORS. Objects may be carried by the wind, and you don't want to be hit.

➡️ The phone should only be used in an emergency. It is important to keep the telephone lines open for people who really need them.

➡️ If you do evacuate, never go back home until local officials say it is safe.

ON YOUR TOES WHEN THE WIND BLOWS

WEB CONNECTIONS

Visit the website **www.fema.gov/kids/dizkit.htm**. Click on "Disaster Supply Kit." With a friend, put together your own disaster supply kit.

19

CYCLONE!

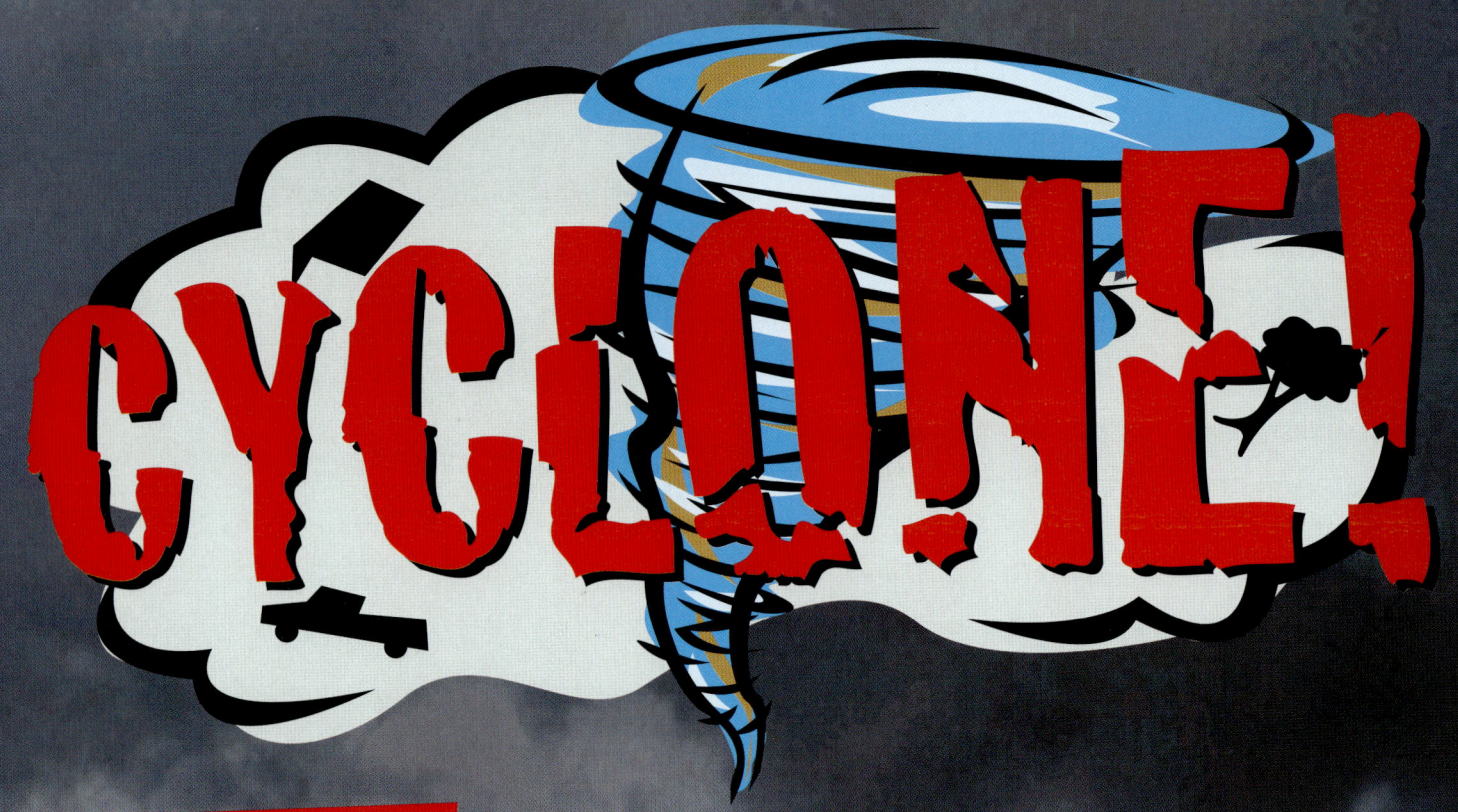

warm up

Cyclones are also known as tornadoes or twisters. Brainstorm other names to describe a cyclone.

In this excerpt from the book, The Wizard of Oz *by L. Frank Baum, Dorothy and her dog Toto are whirled away by a cyclone to a land of fantasy.*

Dorothy lived in the midst of the great Kansas prairies, with Uncle Henry, who was a farmer, and Aunt Em, who was the farmer's wife. Their house was small … There were four walls, a floor, and a roof, which made one room; … There was … a small hole, dug in the ground, called a cyclone cellar, where the family could go in case one of those great whirlwinds arose, mighty enough to crush any building in its path. It was reached by a trap door in the middle of the floor, from which a ladder led down into the small, dark hole.

When Dorothy stood in the doorway and looked around, she could see nothing but the great gray prairie on every side. … The sun had baked the plowed land into a gray mass, with little cracks running through it. Even the grass was not green, for the sun had burned the tops of the long blades until they were the same gray color to be seen everywhere. …

Judy Garland starred as Dorothy in the 1939 movie *The Wizard of Oz*.

> **CHECKPOINT**
> Notice the warning signs that tell Uncle Henry a cyclone is coming.

Uncle Henry sat upon the doorstep and looked *anxiously* at the sky, which was even grayer than usual. Dorothy stood in the door with Toto in her arms, and looked at the sky too. Aunt Em was washing the dishes.

From the far north they heard a low wail of the wind, and Uncle Henry and Dorothy could see where the long grass bowed in waves before the coming storm. There now came a sharp whistling in the air from the south, and as they turned their eyes that way they saw ripples in the grass coming from that direction also.

Suddenly Uncle Henry stood up.

"There's a cyclone coming, Em,"

he called to his wife. "I'll go look after the stock." Then he ran toward the sheds where the cows and horses were kept.

Aunt Em dropped her work and came to the door. One glance told her of the danger close at hand.

"Quick, Dorothy!" she screamed. "Run for the cellar!"

anxiously: nervously

… Aunt Em, badly frightened, threw open the trap door in the floor and climbed down the ladder into the small, dark hole. Dorothy caught Toto at last, and started to follow her aunt. When she was halfway across the room there came a great shriek from the wind, and the house shook so hard that she lost her footing and sat down suddenly upon the floor.

Then a strange thing happened.

The house whirled around two or three times and rose slowly through the air. Dorothy felt as if she were going up in a balloon.

The north and south winds met where the house stood, and made it the exact center of the cyclone. In the middle of a cyclone, the air is generally still, but the great pressure of the wind on every side of the house raised it up higher and higher, until it was at the very top of the cyclone; and there it remained and was carried miles and miles away as easily as you could carry a feather …

wrap up

1. Even though fiction is imaginary, readers can still learn from it. List three things you have learned about cyclones from this excerpt.

2. Write your own ending for this story.

DISASTER AT PINE LAKE

THIS STORY IS BASED ON AN EYEWITNESS ACCOUNT OF A TORNADO THAT HIT PINE LAKE, ALBERTA, ON JULY 14, 2000.

IT WAS SHAPING UP TO BE A GREAT WEEKEND. MY FRIENDS AND I WERE AT THE CABIN WITH NOTHING TO DO BUT HANG OUT. A LITTLE SUN, MAYBE SOME FISHING, A FEW ROUNDS OF GOLF ...

WELL, WILL YOU LOOK AT THAT! WHERE'D ALL THOSE CLOUDS COME FROM?

WE'D BETTER GET THIS STUFF INSIDE. I GIVE IT ABOUT HALF AN HOUR AND WE'RE GONNA GET SOAKED!

THEN IT STARTED. WE HAD NEVER SEEN ANYTHING LIKE IT — THE LAKE HAD GONE A TERRIBLE DARK GRAY. TREES WERE CRASHING TO THE GROUND. ONE LANDED ON DAN'S CAR, AND HE RAN FROM THE CABIN, YELLING ...

DAN! WHERE ARE YOU GOING?!

GET BACK INSIDE OR YOU'LL BE KILLED! COME ON!

AAGGH! I'M COMING BACK IN!

Adapted by PAT CLIFFORD   Illustrated by Mike Rooth

IT WAS THE LONGEST 30 SECONDS OF MY LIFE ...

TORNADO!

EVERYBODY PUSH! PUSH AS HARD AS YOU CAN!

DON'T STOP ... OR IT'LL SUCK US RIGHT OUT OF THE CABIN!

I THINK IT'S PASSED BY ...

AFTERWARD, PEOPLE TOLD US IT TOOK LESS THAN A MINUTE FOR THE TORNADO TO PASS. BUT TO US, IT FELT LIKE A WHOLE LIFETIME.

WHAT ARE YOU DOING?

GOTTA GET THE GAS TURNED OFF ... IF IT STARTS LEAKING, EVERYTHING COULD BLOW SKY HIGH!

WE DECIDED TO TAKE A WALK AROUND THE AREA TO SEE WHAT HAPPENED ...
IF THE BARBECUE IS STILL ON, WHAT HAPPENED TO THE PEOPLE?
LOOK AT THIS! THE THING'S STILL ON — HOW CAN THIS HAPPEN?
PLEASE HELP US! WE NEED FIRST AID! DO YOU HAVE BANDAGES? ANYTHING?!?
THERE'S A KIT IN THE BACK OF MY NEIGHBOR'S TRUCK ...
FOUND IT! COME ON, LET'S GO!
FIRST AID
YOU GUYS BETTER PREPARE YOURSELVES ...
... IT'S WAY WORSE THAN ANYTHING I'VE EVER SEEN ...
OH MY GOSH ... I THINK PEOPLE MIGHT HAVE DIED HERE.
ALL WE COULD DO WAS STAND THERE, HELPLESS. IT WAS SO QUIET. EXCEPT INSIDE. INSIDE I WAS SCREAMING -- SCREAMING FOR WORDS TO DESCRIBE THE STORM. HOW COULD THIS HAPPEN? HOW COULD IT EVEN BE REAL?

"MY KIDS! I CAN'T FIND MY KIDS!!"

"HAVE YOU SEEN MY KIDS? THEY WERE WITH MY DAD ... THEY WERE ONLY A COUPLE OF MINUTES AHEAD OF ME WHEN IT HIT ..."

"MY BABIES! ..."

"DADDY!!"

"OH MAN, I'VE NEVER SEEN ANYTHING MORE BEAUTIFUL THAN THAT."

I DON'T KNOW WHY WE DID IT, BUT WE ALL BENT OVER AND PICKED UP A GOLF BALL ...

MAYBE IT WAS A REMINDER OF THAT DAY. MAYBE IT WAS A REMINDER OF HOW LUCKY WE WERE TO BE SPARED.

wrap up

Most natural disasters affect ordinary people. Yet people find strength to cope. With a partner, create a newspaper article about how someone survived a tornado or another natural disaster.

FIGHTING FOREST FIRES

By Cayley Mackay

warm up

In some U.S. states, decisions on how to fight a fire are mostly made using a computer program. Do you think this is a good idea? With a partner, discuss whether you would prefer to rely on human experience or technology.

MARIEVE

MATT

Cayley Mackay is 13 years old. She lived for 11 years at a Ranger Station and her home has always been in a forest. Some of her favorite people are firefighters. She wants to work as a ranger and a volunteer firefighter some day.

In this interview, Cayley talks to Marieve and Matt about their jobs. They are firefighters who work on forest fires.

CAYLEY: What skills do you need for the job?

MARIEVE: You have to be smart to stay safe. You have to be able to solve problems. You have to realize that you are playing with fire.

Next you need to be in great shape. To get hired you need to pass a physical test. I had to walk 3 miles in 45 minutes with a 45 lb. pack on my back. Right after the walk, I had to lift a 52 lb. barbell, 18 times. Then I had to run the timed course with a hose and pump. You have to pass this test, two to three times a season.

You also need good social skills. Not just for the public you meet but with your crew. You eat, live, work, and party together. Often you don't get a break from your crew for 22 days.

CAYLEY: Marieve, you are on the Initial Attack Crew. What does that mean?

MARIEVE: It means that I work on a crew of four people and usually we are the first ones sent to a fire. When a call comes in, we quickly get our gear and then wait for directions. Sometimes we will work on the fire until it is extinguished, like when it is a small fire. With a bigger fire, we work on it until another crew comes in. Then we leave, so that we can be ready if another fire comes up.

> **CHECKPOINT**
> Why would more than one crew have to be sent to fight a fire?

CAYLEY: Matt? Do you like helicopters? What was your job in the helicopter?

MATT: I do like riding in a helicopter! My job in the helicopter depended a lot on where I was sitting. For instance, while on a patrol, the people at the window seats have to be watching for "smokes."

CAYLEY: What type of methods and equipment do you use to fight a wildfire?

MARIEVE: It kind of depends on the fire. If it is a small fire we use hand tools, like a Pulaski, which is a kind

In 2003, British Columbia experienced 2,460 forest fires. The fires destroyed 617,775 acres of land. Three people died as a result of the fire, and 334 homes were destroyed.

In 2003, California lost 750,000 acres of land, 3,700 homes and 24 lives. 6,000 California firefighters and 8,000 out-of-state firefighters were called in to fight the out-of-control blazes.

of ax with a rake on the other side. But for big fires we might use a pump and a lot of hose, shovels, helicopters that have drop buckets for water, air tankers, dozers, fire trucks, etc.

MATT: The sort of methods and equipment you use depends on the size of the fire, the landscape, where water is, the weather, and how the fire is acting. Different people, tools, and attack methods will be used in different situations.

CAYLEY: What do you see when you're on the scene of a forest fire?

MARIEVE: Lots of different things like helicopters, airplanes dropping retardant, and lots of people helping one another. We work side by side putting out the fire; big friendships happen when we work side by side.

MATT: Usually, you see at least smoke. Sometimes that's all. Other times there are a lot of flames with the smoke. Sometimes there's a big burn scar showing where the fire has been. Other times it's just a smoke plume in a forest of green trees.

retardant: *material that won't burn*
plume: *a long spreading cloud of smoke*

In 2004, Alaska had 703 forest fires. Over 6 million acres of land were burned.

The biggest thing for me about a fire is the smell. There's nothing that smells like the forest burning. The smell isn't like a campfire, it's like life on fire. The mixture of what you see and smell makes you think about the life of the fire and the death of the forest.

CAYLEY: What do you do when you arrive at a fire?

MARIEVE: We make sure we are safe when we get out of the helicopter. We have a system called L.A.C.E.S. which means we put **L**ookouts, we have an **A**nchor point, we check out our **C**ommunication systems, we have an **E**scape route, and we plan our **S**afety zone to be ready if something unpredictable happens.

CHECKPOINT
Notice how the firefighters protect themselves while doing their job.

After that, we get the equipment out. The pump comes out; then we lay the hose, and then we get our hand tools. Sometimes we use a chainsaw to cut logs to make a helipad so that a helicopter can land. We also cut down dangerous trees.

Once everything is good and the smoke is out, we will be cold trailing. That is when we touch the ground with our hand to make sure the ground where the fire was is cold. If it isn't, we add more water and dig deeper.

CAYLEY: How do most wildfires start?

MARIEVE: It really depends where you are. Around the mountains, most fires seem to be started by careless people who didn't put out their campfires, or careless smokers who throw cigarette butts. Sometimes, fires might start with carbons sparking out of an ATV (all-terrain vehicle). Outside of the mountains, lightning starts most fires.

FYI

When a fire is started on purpose to help keep an ecosystem in balance, it is called a "prescribed burn." This is not a new idea. Aboriginal peoples around the world used to light fires to make more grasslands for game or to clear roads for traveling. Early explorers and trappers also started fires for the same reasons.

CHECKPOINT
How can fire be good for the forest?

wrap up

1. Cayley asked questions that would help her understand what it was like fighting forest fires. Do you think she did a good job? Give reasons for your answer.

2. With a partner, create a brochure to prevent forest fires. Use information from this interview in your brochure.

CAYLEY: What happens with the wild animals when there is a fire?

MATT: Most animals know a fire has started and will start leaving.

CAYLEY: Some people think that wildfires are a good thing in a forest and that we should let wildfires burn. Why would a fire be a good thing?

MARIEVE: Fire is really important for the ecosystem. Often, trees need to burn in order for new things to grow in the forest. For example, the cones of Black Spruce and Lodge Pole Pine will only open with the intense heat of fire. Then the seeds fall out of their cones. Those kinds of trees grow tight together, like they are waiting for fire to catch them.

MATT: Fire can be a good thing as it renews all of the forest. It brings some animals back, too, that are unable to live in a single aged forest, an old growth forest, or a forest that is too thick.

Fire also reduces the fire hazard. If a forest has gone for years and years without a fire, and one starts, it will be impossible to put out. But if fire is allowed to be a regular part of the ecosystem, then the fires are usually smaller. I believe to have a healthy forest, you need to have old and new growth. To have a healthy forest, you need to have fires.

CAYLEY: Merci Marieve! Thanks Matt!

---

ecosystem: *the system of interactions between living organisms and their environment*
renews: *make new again*

→ Make sure your house has a working smoke detector on every floor. Have your parents check to make sure that all of the detectors work. You should also have one working fire extinguisher.

→ Create a fire plan of how to escape from your house if it is on fire.

→ If you are caught in a fire, follow these steps:
- Stay low to the ground where the smoke is not so heavy.
- NEVER hide during a fire. Always get out.
- Once you are out, stay out. Never go back for a toy or anything else.
- Tell an adult if there is a person left behind in the burning house.

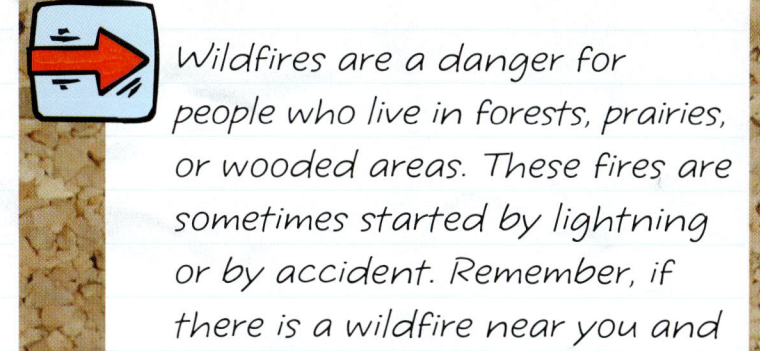

→ Wildfires are a danger for people who live in forests, prairies, or wooded areas. These fires are sometimes started by lightning or by accident. Remember, if there is a wildfire near you and your family is told to evacuate — go right away!

FYI

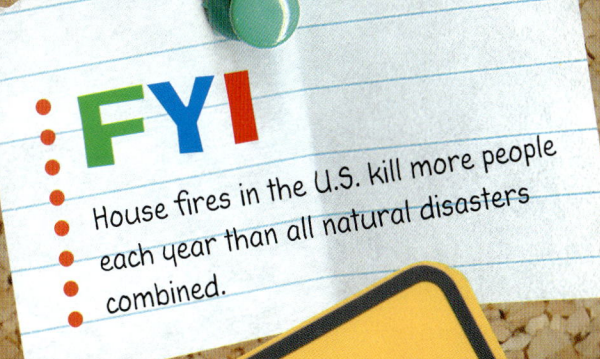

House fires in the U.S. kill more people each year than all natural disasters combined.

STAYING COOL WHEN IT'S HOT

WEB CONNECTIONS

Using the Internet, research a forest fire that took place during the past summer. Use this information to write a newspaper report for your school newspaper.

FLOOD OF '94

By Debra Kaufman

> **warm up**
>
> Have you ever heard the phrase, "hope against hope"? Talk about a time when you felt this way.

We'd seen high water before
but never like this.
My husband, waist-deep in it,
came in from the barn shivering:
"We'll have to go upstairs now."
The sky never looked so close.
Dirty water rushed below us,
pieces of fence we'd just mended
and my best tin bucket.

He said, "Don't you dare cry."
He meant, "Something has to be held back."
The house trembled from the wrath.
We knew then we had to leave.
Our home. Our farm.
Our heifers bawling, "Ma, Ma."
Bob Lucas came by in his tractor and took us away.
By then the water was up to the cows' chins.
They don't like the wet, the cold;
it makes them want to lie down and sleep.

CHECKPOINT
"Our home. Our farm." These are the shortest sentences in the poem. Why do you think the author wrote them like that?

It was two days before we could come back.
I'd already imagined the worst:
I don't hope against hope.
And there they were, our beautiful Jerseys.
They bellowed to us, eyes wide.
They licked our hands.
Somehow Marianne had birthed a new calf.
We named her Miracle. We'll keep her forever.
We rolled up our sleeves and milked them underwater.

heifers: *young cows*

CHECKPOINT
The author says she doesn't hope against hope, so she went back to imagining the worst. Do you agree that's the best way to face a disaster?

wrap up

Poets think in images, which are pictures they paint with words. Which word pictures in this poem do you think would make fantastic artwork? Try drawing or painting one of them.

Illustration by Jane Ray

FLOOD FACTS

warm up

Have you ever seen news reports on floods? What happens to the people in the area? Discuss in a small group.

FYI

About two-thirds of rainwater evaporates. The rest of the water falls into two categories:

1. Controllable runoff – This is water that flows into rivers and lakes.

2. Uncontrollable runoff – This water causes floods. It flows towards the already-filled lakes and rivers.

wrap up

1. With a partner, create a flow chart titled "The Water Cycle" and explain the flood cycle.

2. People know that rivers overflow. But, many people choose to live near rivers and oceans anyway. Why do you think this is? With a partner make up a list with five good reasons.

Water is important to all living things. We drink it. We use it to wash, to clean, and to grow food. Water is usually not dangerous when it is controlled. But when water becomes unruly, it can be deadly.

Floodwaters are dangerous for two main reasons. For one thing, water is very heavy. Heavy things can do a lot of damage. Think about a bucket of water. Now think about letting the water flow out, just a little at a time, on top of a tall sandcastle. When your bucket is empty, part of the castle might still be there. Now, if you dumped the whole bucket on the castle at one time, the castle would disappear a lot faster.

Floods happen every year because of heavy rainfalls. Most of the rain evaporates into the air or is absorbed by soil and plants. The rain that does not evaporate or soak into the earth runs into streams, rivers, lakes, and the ocean. Once it gets back to the ocean, it evaporates back into the air and the whole process starts again.

evaporates: turns from liquid to vapour
absorbed: soaked up

CHECKPOINT

Think about a bathtub. If you forget to turn off the tap, the bathtub will overflow once it is full. The same thing happens to lakes and rivers.

RIVER OF SORROW
Northern China, 1887

Life was tough for the Chinese peasant farmers who lived beside the mighty Yellow River. No matter how hard they worked each day in the fields below the river, they barely produced enough food to feed their families.

September 1887 saw a month of almost non-stop rain. The river had begun to rise and people feared that it would burst its banks.

Over the centuries, the Yellow River had flooded the flatlands of China's Great Plain more than 1,500 times. The river had claimed so many lives and caused such tremendous suffering that it was known as "China's Sorrow."

Despite the threat of flooding, no one thought to leave. This was their home. Their families had lived there for hundreds of years. It was also harvest time — they would starve if they did not bring in their crops soon.

warm up
Looking at the title of this article, what do you think it will be about?

CHECKPOINT
What kept these people from leaving?

FYI

- Since 1887, the Yellow River has flooded many times. In 1991, 1,270 people drowned and two million were left homeless.

- Drinking water that contained dangerous substances caused by the flood led to disease.

CHECKPOINT
Why would the sharp bend in the river cause such a problem for flooding?

wrap up

Imagine that you survived this flood. Write a journal entry describing your experiences.

The rain continued to fall, and the river rose higher and higher. In some places, it was already 16 ft. above the flat lands. While some peasants gathered in the harvest, others set to work building **embankments** alongside the river. These embankments, called dikes, were their only hope of holding back the water.

But it was no use. At a sharp bend near the city of Zhengzhou, the fast-flowing river finally swelled over its banks. It tore over a half-mile-long gap in the dikes, pouring a **torrent** of water onto the Great Plain.

The flood swept away the peasants in the fields, but their cries were not heard above the noise of the rushing water. As the torrent reached the villages beyond the river, people climbed onto their roofs for safety. Some braved the flood in boats or rafts, rescuing people or throwing food to those **marooned** by the raging water.

The flood covered 11 cities and 1,500 villages and killed 900,000 people. Thousands more died of disease and starvation. It took 18 months to fix the dikes and bring the river back under control.

Today, the flood defenses along the Yellow River are much improved. Dynamite has been used to alter the river's course to avoid dangerous bends, and plans have been made to build a huge, powerful dam. But the river will never be completely tamed. "China's Sorrow" will surely claim many more victims.

---

embankments: *low walls*   **marooned:** *isolated*
torrent: *gush, flood*

➡️ Try your best to stay away from flood water. This water can be contaminated (contain dangerous substances).

➡️ Never walk through moving water. Moving water is very strong, so it could knock you off your feet. If you must walk through water, always walk where the water is not moving. Use a stick to test the ground in front of you.

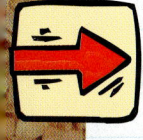

➡️ Stay far away from power lines that are on the ground.

➡️ Listen to radio updates on a battery-powered radio.

FYI

In 2004, 114 people were killed and dozens were reported missing after heavy rains swamped the southwest region of China.

Floods destroy homes and crops. Some have wiped out entire villages.

KEEP YOUR HEAD ABOVE WATER

WEB CONNECTIONS

Some of the most famous rivers in the world also have a long history of disastrous flooding. Using the Internet, find out about one of those rivers and write your own story about the disaster.

China Flood—CORBIS

MILLIONS OF LIVES AT RISK

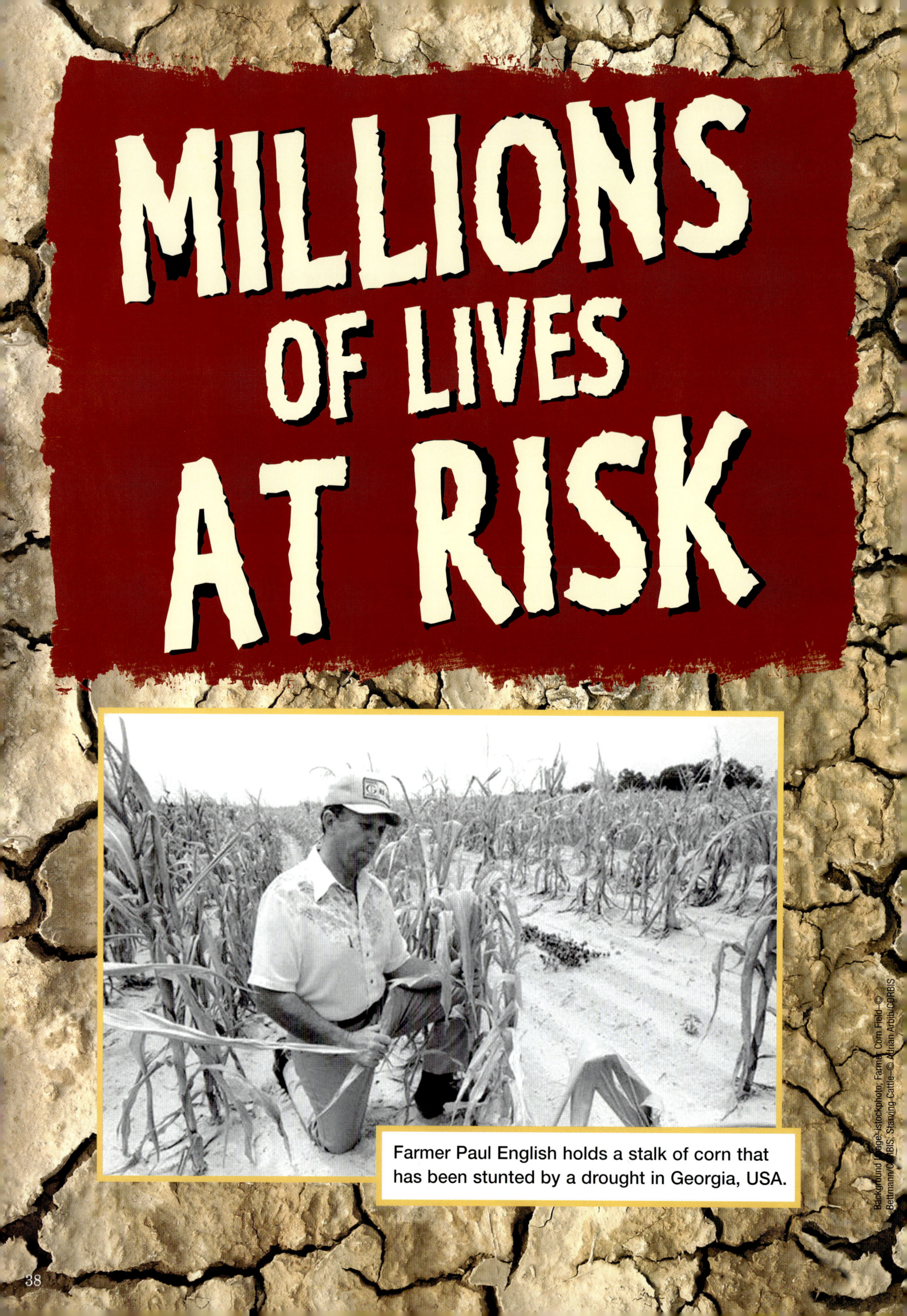

Farmer Paul English holds a stalk of corn that has been stunted by a drought in Georgia, USA.

Droughts are the most stubborn of natural disasters. They can last longer and cover larger areas than hurricanes, tornadoes, floods, and earthquakes.

A drought is a serious shortage of water, caused by a lack of rainfall over a long period of time. Serious droughts can result in food shortages and damage to the natural landscape, which directly affects wildlife.

WORLD WATER COUNCIL WARNING: "Droughts are becoming more severe and widespread. Up to 45% of reported deaths from natural disasters between 1992 and 2001 resulted from droughts and famines."

In November 2004, farmers in Guangxi, China reported "drought destroyed 1,500 acres of crops, mainly rice and sugarcane. Farmers in some of the hardest-hit villages will not harvest enough grain to feed even themselves."

— *The China Daily*

FYI

- In 2002, the BBC reported that 12.8 million people from southern Africa were on the verge of starvation caused by a drought that had destroyed crops and killed livestock.
- In 2003, extreme heat and drought caused 20,000 deaths in Europe.

warm up

Can you recall a time when it didn't rain for many days? What happened?

CHECKPOINT

How could a drought damage the landscape? Why would this affect wildlife?

Cattle weakened by a long spell of drought in northern Kenya.

This is how life changed for people living in Virginia during a drought in 2002.

Fitness centers installed water-saving shower heads and posted signs asking members to limit their showers to two minutes each.

Hotels used recycled water from washing machines to mop floors. They also cut back on the number of laundry loads they did each day.

Decorative water fountains were shut off throughout the city. Lawn watering was stopped completely.

To save water when washing dishes, restaurants switched to paper plates. Some restaurants even set up outhouses so that customers would not need to use flush toilets.

Signs were posted in bathrooms reminding people not to flush unless necessary. Students were told not to wash their hands after using the washroom; instead they used hand sanitizers.

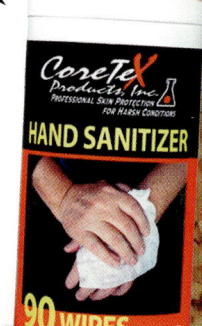

wrap up

With a partner, brainstorm ways life would change for you if severe water restrictions were put in place. Share your views with the class.

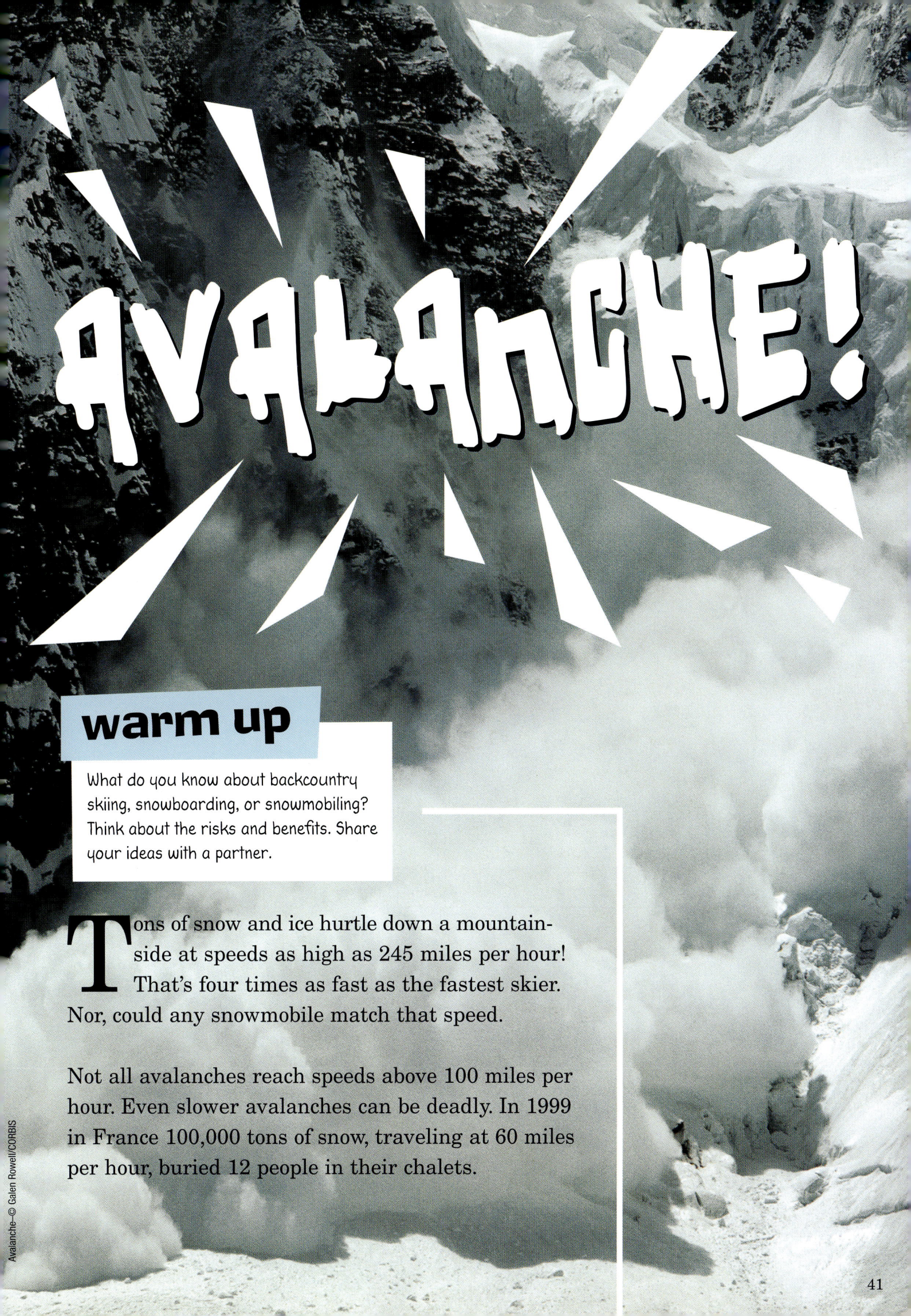

AVALANCHE!

warm up

What do you know about backcountry skiing, snowboarding, or snowmobiling? Think about the risks and benefits. Share your ideas with a partner.

Tons of snow and ice hurtle down a mountainside at speeds as high as 245 miles per hour! That's four times as fast as the fastest skier. Nor, could any snowmobile match that speed.

Not all avalanches reach speeds above 100 miles per hour. Even slower avalanches can be deadly. In 1999 in France 100,000 tons of snow, traveling at 60 miles per hour, buried 12 people in their chalets.

FYI

- Approximately 150 deaths are reported each year by the 17 countries that are members of the International Commission for Alpine Rescue; 85 % of these deaths occur in the Alps.

Weather conditions, the height of a mountain, the steepness of a mountain slope, the type of snow, and construction in the area are all factors that contribute to avalanches. Today, however, most avalanches are triggered by noise and movement made by people enjoying recreational activities. In British Columbia, Canada two avalanches, 12 days apart in 2003, killed 14 skiers and snowboarders — including U.S. snowboard pioneer Craig Kelly.

France, Austria, Switzerland, and Italy experience the highest number of avalanches and the most deaths from avalanches. The United States is fifth worldwide, with Colorado being the most dangerous state.

Worst Avalanche Disaster in the US.

In 1910, a train carrying 150 passengers was trapped by snow in the Cascades Mountains in Washington State. All were killed when an avalanche swept the train into a gorge over 150 feet below.

Worst Avalanche Disaster in the World

In 1962, nearly 4,000 people were killed by an avalanche in the Andes in Peru.

wrap up

You are a TV reporter. Write three questions that you would ask someone who experienced an avalanche.

➡️ Be prepared — take a training course, and carry a beacon, *probes*, and a shovel.

probes: **long object used for exploring under the snow**

➡️ Stay calm and don't panic. Instead of trying to outrun an avalanche, try to move as close to the edge of the avalanche as possible or grab a hold of a tree.

➡️ Swing your arms forward (in a swimming motion). This will help to keep you near the surface.

➡️ Get rid of any equipment you may have on you, like skis, snowboards, or snowshoes. All of these things are heavy and could pull you deeper into the snow. They could also cause more injuries as you tumble.

➡️ When the tumbling slows down, protect your airway. Hold your hands in front of your face to make an air pocket.

➡️ If you can move, hold one arm over your head. This will help rescuers to find you.

AVALANCHE SURVIVAL TIPS

43

Wave of Te...

warm up

Study the images on this page. With a partner, brainstorm words and phrases to describe the scene.

On December 26, 2004 a wave of terror slammed down on Indonesia, Sri Lanka, South India, and Thailand — killing more than 200,000 people. This tsunami, which originated in the Indian Ocean, is being called the deadliest disaster of modern times.

A tsunami (pronounced soo-nahm-ee) is a series of huge waves that happen after an undersea disturbance, such as an earthquake or volcano eruption. (Tsunami is from the Japanese word for harbor wave.) The waves travel in all directions from the area of disturbance, much like the ripples that happen after throwing a rock. The waves may travel in the open sea as fast as 450 miles per hour. As the big waves approach shallow waters along the coast they grow to a great height and smash into the shore. They can be as high as 100 feet. They can cause a lot of destruction on the shore. They are sometimes mistakenly called "tidal waves," but tsunami have nothing to do with the tides.

Hawaii is the state at greatest risk for a tsunami. They get about one a year, with a damaging tsunami happening about every seven years. Alaska is also at high risk. California, Oregon, and Washington experience a damaging tsunami about every 18 years.

The Tsunami Warning Centers in Honolulu Hawaii, and Palmer Alaska monitor disturbances that might trigger tsunami. When a tsunami is recorded, the center tracks it and issues a warning when needed.

CHECKPOINT

Notice how fast the waves can be. Compare this with the speed of a car.

FYI

In 1964, an Alaskan earthquake generated a tsunami with waves between 10 and 20 feet high along parts of the California, Oregon, and Washington coasts.

Dramatic photo taken by a tourist at Kamala Beach Hotel in Phuket, Thailand, as tsunami waves sweep into the area, December 26, 2004.

A mother cries near the bodies of her children, killed in the tsunami, as they lay on the floor of a hospital in Southern India, December 27, 2004.

FYI

The December 2004 Indian Ocean tsunami was said to have waves as high as 50 feet in some places. That's the equivalent of a six-story building.

As many as one-third of the people who died in the Indian Ocean tsunami were children because they were not strong enough to fight against the powerful force of the water.

Thai Child Survivors Face the Future

By Kate McGeown **March 29, 2005, BBC News**

The Navarak family can usually be found in their small hut in Khuk Khak refugee camp — along with many other Thais who lost their homes in December's tsunami.

But for most of last Thursday, eight-year-old Anasorn was missing. He had fled to the hills earlier in the day after a tsunami warning, and only returned several hours later.

"He's still really scared," said Anasorn's father Thoon Navarak. "Whenever there's a rumor about another wave, he runs away and doesn't come back for ages."

"He survived the tsunami by floating on a piece of wood. He climbed up a tree, but when the water went down again he had to wait several hours before he was rescued. It's not something he can just forget." …

Various aid agencies have set up child-*oriented* centers in some of the camps for those made homeless in the disaster.

"With the little children, we spend time singing and painting. But with older children, we just talk to them about their problems," said Phakamas Kamcham, a staff member at the center in Thaptawan camp.

"They are gradually getting over it," she said, "but they will never forget."

> **CHECKPOINT**
> As you read notice how the agencies are helping children. How do the children react?

"One thing we're really trying to encourage them to do is go back to the sea," she said.

"To start with we just took them to the beach to see the sunset. Then the staff went swimming, and finally some of the children did as well."

But for some, the sea is still a dangerous place.

---

oriented: aimed at

Udon Pradit said his 13-year-old son Manroit was unable to go anywhere near the beach. "He has nightmares about it," he said.

Three-year-old Charnathip is also afraid of the sea, even though he was far away when the tsunami happened.

"When we got back home, he ran in to what remained of our house before we could stop him, and he saw the dead bodies of his cousin and his uncle," said Charnathip's mother Songdao Ponkaen.

"Only yesterday he asked if the tsunami was coming back again."

wrap up

1. Imagine how Anasorn felt waiting in the tree until the water went down. Share your thoughts with a partner.

2. Using the images of the tsunami and the information in this article, write a script for a radio or TV broadcast from one of the countries hit by the tsunami on December 26, 2004.

WEB CONNECTIONS

Visit **www.fema.gov/kids** to find out the type of work FEMA (Federal Emergency Management Agency) does during disasters. Report your findings to the class.

Indonesian children smile and cheer as U.S. Navy helicopters fly in purified water and relief supplies to a small village on the Island of Sumatra, Indonesia.

ACKNOWLEDGMENTS

The publisher gratefully acknowledges the following for permission to reprint copyrighted material in this book.

Every reasonable effort has been made to trace the owners of copyrighted material and to make due acknowledgment. Any errors or omissions drawn to our attention will be gladly rectified in future editions.

"Pelee Awakes" and "River of Sorrow" from *Volcanoes and Other Natural Disasters* by Harriet Giffrey is used with permission of Dorling Kindersley, London © 1998.

"The Flood of '94" © 1997 Debra Kaufman.

"Thai child survivors face the future" by Kate McGeown. Permission to reprint courtesy of BBC News at bbcnews.com.

"Strange, but True" and "The Water Cycle" from *Hurricane* by Carl Meister is used with permission of Abdo and Daughters Publishing, Minnesota © 1999.

"Quake Shakes 'Frisco" from *Earthquake!* by Cynthia Pratt Nicolson is used with permission of Kids Can Press Ltd., Toronto. Text © 2002 Cynthia Pratt Nicolson.

"Wave of Terror" excerpt from "Tsunami" at www.fema.gov/kids/tsunami.htm. Permission to reprint couresty of Federal Emergency Management Agency.